2257-01 © 2024 Highlights for Children, Inc.

T0012515

Monster Olympics Live!
pages 4–5

Halloween Night
pages 6–7

Lost in Transit
pages 8–9

"Trick or Cheese!"
pages 10–11

Cat Karaoke
pages 12–13

Pumpkin Hauling
pages 14–15

Scared in Transylvania
pages 16–17

A Special Birthday
pages 18–19

A Monster Sale
pages 20–21

banana | snow cone | bacon | lollipop | ring
ladle | pennant | cupcake | chili pepper | spool of thread

Goopy Scoops
pages 22–23

key | teddy bear | magnet | lemon | comb
pencil | fork | fried egg | swim fin | book

Ghostly Games
pages 24–25

baseball bat | football | glove | sock | comb
cactus | domino | bowl | spoon | artist's brush

Cauldron Contest
pages 26–27

truck | snowman | mitten | ladder | teacup
ice-cream cone | crayon | bread | ring | saucepan

The Spooky Salon
pages 28–29

wrench | light bulb | safety pin | tweezers | tent
canoe | necktie | acorn | saltshaker | ladybug

Happy Hauntings
pages 30–31

drumstick | pizza | hanger | artist's brush | toothbrush
flashlight | teapot | toothpaste | fish | slipper

A Ghostly Outing
pages 32–33

megaphone | crescent moon | fork | sock | pizza
glove | flashlight | yo-yo | toothbrush | fish

Perfect Party
pages 34–35

cheese | goggles | pie | green bean | domino
cinnamon bun | pennant | toothbrush | comb | french fry

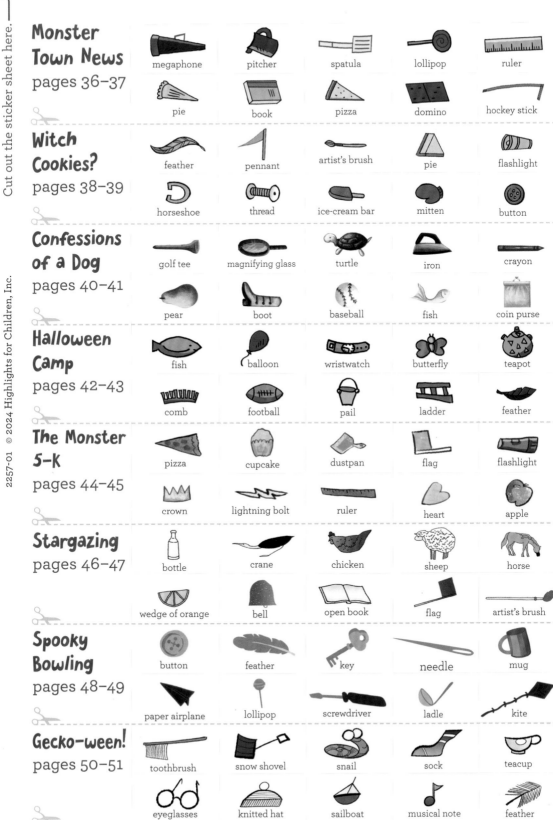

Monster Town News
pages 36–37

megaphone · pitcher · spatula · lollipop · ruler
pie · book · pizza · domino · hockey stick

Witch Cookies?
pages 38–39

feather · pennant · artist's brush · pie · flashlight
horseshoe · thread · ice-cream bar · mitten · button

Confessions of a Dog
pages 40–41

golf tee · magnifying glass · turtle · iron · crayon
pear · boot · baseball · fish · coin purse

Halloween Camp
pages 42–43

fish · balloon · wristwatch · butterfly · teapot
comb · football · pail · ladder · feather

The Monster 5-K
pages 44–45

pizza · cupcake · dustpan · flag · flashlight
crown · lightning bolt · ruler · heart · apple

Stargazing
pages 46–47

bottle · crane · chicken · sheep · horse
wedge of orange · bell · open book · flag · artist's brush

Spooky Bowling
pages 48–49

button · feather · key · needle · mug
paper airplane · lollipop · screwdriver · ladle · kite

Gecko-ween!
pages 50–51

toothbrush · snow shovel · snail · sock · teacup
eyeglasses · knitted hat · sailboat · musical note · feather

Monster Mash
pages 52–53

hockey stick · cauliflower · adhesive bandage · waffle · ruler
bell · chili pepper · crown · drumstick · domino

The Largest Pumpkin
pages 54–55

crown · musical note · needle · spatula · teacup
ring · pie · pointy hat · toothbrush · ice-cream soda

Campfire Tales
pages 56–57

football · football helmet · artist's brush · paper clip · fish
bell · chili pepper · pizza · spoon · pie

Monster's Bash
pages 58–59

mitten · ladybug · pennant · worm · spoon
present · crown · hat · teacup · pea pod

Spook-tacular Halloween!
page 60

cat · ghost · candy · flashlight · frog
candy corn · candy · crow · boo! · bat
mouse · candy corn · boo! · spiderweb · potion
pumpkin · treat bag · boo! · crow · mask
spider · lollipop · cat · witch's broom · spiderweb
lollipop · cat · bat · candy · ghost
treat bag · pumpkin · mask · potion · mouse
spell book · mask · lollipop · bat · pirate hat

Highlights

Silly Sticker
STORIES
HALLOWEEN

HIGHLIGHTS PRESS
Honesdale, Pennsylvania

Create your own silly story!

Each Hidden Pictures puzzle in this book comes with a story for you to finish. Use the sticker sheets to start puzzling!

Here's what you do:

2 Peel the sticker.

1 Find a hidden object.

3 Place it in the story.

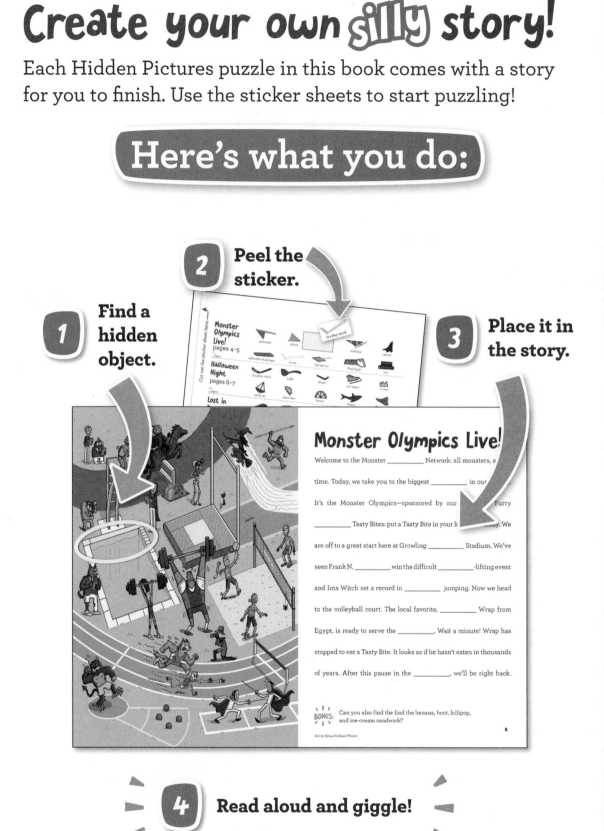

4 Read aloud and giggle!

Contents

Monster Olympics Live!

Welcome to the Monster _____ Network: all monsters, all the time. Today, we take you to the biggest _____ in our history. It's the Monster Olympics—sponsored by our friends at Furry _____ Tasty Bites: put a Tasty Bite in your lunchbox today. We are off to a great start here at Growling _____ Stadium. We've seen Frank N. _____ win the difficult _____-lifting event and Ima Witch set a record in _____ jumping. Now we head to the volleyball court. The local favorite, _____ Wrap from Egypt, is ready to serve the _____. Wait a minute! Wrap has stopped to eat a Tasty Bite. It looks as if he hasn't eaten in thousands of years. After this pause in the _____, we'll be right back.

BONUS: Can you also find the find the banana, boot, lollipop, and ice-cream sandwich?

Art by Brian Michael Weaver

Halloween Night

Have you ever heard the expression, "Trick or treat, smell my

_____"? I think that's kind of mean. After all, if people are

giving me candy to put in my _____, I want to be nice to them!

This year, my best buddy, Henry, put a squishy _____ on

his head and pretended to be an old _____. He is hilarious!

I decided to wear a green crown and hold a big _____. Get

it? I'm the Statue of _____! Henry and I and a bunch of

friends went trick-or-treating together. I think our neighbors

liked seeing us standing on their _____, especially Mr.

_____. He handed me a sugarcoated _____—my

favorite! I said thanks, and then I ate the whole thing before we got

to the next _____. I mean, that's the polite thing to do, right?

BONUS: Can you also find the comb, hammer, and fishhook?

Lost in Transit

Last night, I thought I was as lost as a stray _____ in a

strange _____. I flew in circles over the town of West

_____ for hours looking for the _____ party I was

attending. I was supposed to be the party's honored _____!

But every time I glanced down from the _____ I was riding

on, I could see only towering _____ trees. Then my cat, Mr.

Fuzzy Fluffkins, meowed at me. "Oh, right!" I replied. I grabbed my

big _____ that was hanging nearby. I opened it and grabbed

my bewitched _____ phone. After pressing a few buttons,

I was back on track! I gave Mr. Fluffkins an extra big helping of

ground-up _____ at the party to say thank you.

BONUS: Can you also find the worm, banana, ruler, toothbrush, and fried egg?

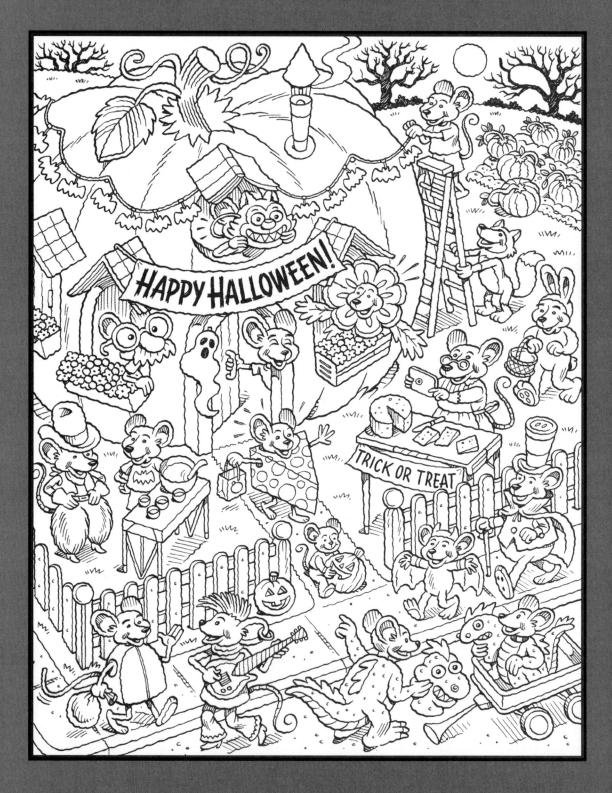

"Trick or Cheese!"

Halloween in Mouseville is anything but boring. First of all, there

is the _____ -decorating contest. This year, my mom stuck a

chocolate-covered _____ on our front door! Then there is the

neighborhood party, where everyone carves a giant _____

and then eats a _____ stuffed with apple butter. But my

favorite part of Halloween here is trick-or-treating. Not only do we

get candy, but people also hand out all kinds of cheese, including

my favorite: Swiss _____. This year, I'm dressing up as Count

_____. I bet I'll be the only vampire with a _____ on

his head! My two best buddies are dressing as a pair of _____

and _____ shakers. We're going to have more fun than a

_____ at a circus! Happy Halloween!

BONUS: Can you also find the open book, crown, sailboat, and slice of pie?

Cat Karaoke

Come on down to Cat Karaoke this October. Just like last month,

DJ "_____ Whiskers" will be playing the best _____

music to yowl to. That includes the spooky hit song by The Catnip

_____. If you're more in a purring mood, don't worry, we'll

have slow favorites like, "No Furball in My _____." The cat

with the best karaoke voice will win a stay at the _____ Hotel

and a new Ace 100 _____ to keep their claws sharp and shiny.

Maybe eating is more your thing than singing. No *purr*-blem! There

will be _____-flavored crunchy mice, fish with _____

sauce, and wild _____ stew. So wash your whiskers, put on

your fanciest _____, and come on down!

BONUS: Can you also find the peanut, baseball, slice of pizza, and arrow?

Pumpkin Hauling

Every year, my family gets in our four-wheel-drive _____

and heads to Bo's Supersized _____ and Pumpkin Patch. And

every year, I get stuck carrying the heaviest _____. All while

my charming little sister watches me heave and haul—without even

offering to lend a _____. The other bad thing about Bo's is

that there's no squishy _____ to wallow in. It's hard to go so

long without rubbing my hoof in a _____ puddle or at least

on a damp _____. But it means a lot to Dad to find the perfect

_____ for Halloween. So I pick up a giant pumpkin that

weighs more than a _____. Then my sister says to me, "When

we get home, you can be first to jump in the muddy _____."

Maybe she isn't so bad after all!

BONUS: Can you also find the mushroom, banana, nail, musical note, wishbone, drinking straw, crescent moon, shoe, button, and artist's brush?

Scared In Transylvania

I am a vampire, and Halloween scares me. My brother thinks this

is hilarious. "You'd better get into your _____ and pull the

_____ over your head until November," he says. Nothing

scares him. Not even a black _____ crossing his path while

he walks under a _____! Mom says I need to face my fears.

She is making me decorate the _____ for Halloween. We

have super scary _____ decorations—like a coffin with a

_____ on it and a skull with a _____ dripping from its

eyes. But I tell Mom I'll try. Then Dad gives me some advice. "When

you see a scary _____, picture it wearing a clown's nose."

I picture a giant _____ clown and giggle. Maybe I can get

through Halloween after all!

BONUS: Can you also find the baseball cap, slice of pie, fishhook, carrot, and heart?

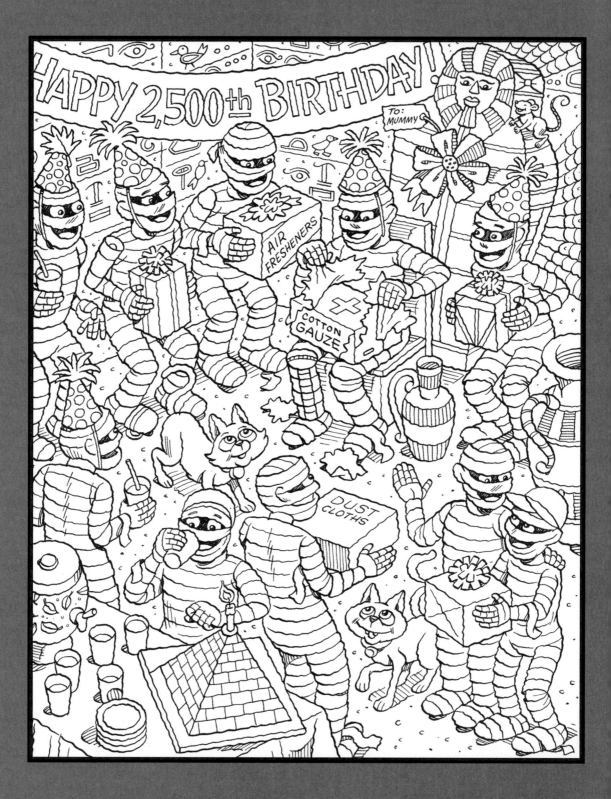

A Special Birthday

"Happy _____ Day to me! I'm an ancient mummy!" That's

my favorite song. I sing it every year on October 31st—my birthday.

That's when my friends throw me a big _____ party, complete

with cake made from a tasty _____, a punch bowl filled with

a _____ and dry ice, and a mound of gifts. We mummies

know how to party! Before I open my first _____, everyone

hits the dance floor. I do the _____ Boogie. When my favorite

song, "Wrap It Up," comes on, I jump up onto the _____ and

show my best moves. After that, I need a break. I open my gifts and

unwrap a ticket to ride a _____ all the way to the North Pole!

I've always wanted to see a _____ bear. I sure am a lucky

_____!

BONUS: Can you also find the screw, bowl, banana, flashlight, and leaf?

A Monster Sale

Halloween is two days away, and I still need a costume. I want to

dress up like a _____ chief. My little sister thinks being

a fairy _____ would be more fun. I was planning to make

my own costume out of a cardboard _____, a flashing

_____, and a hard plastic _____. But just try to find

all that in our house—no way. Luckily, Dad brought us to a new

_____ shop nearby that's having a sale on costumes. The

store is fantastic! Right away, I found the _____ I'd been

trying to find. But as I watched my sister prance around with

a _____ on her head, I got an idea. My sister and I could

be a really funny _____ set. I asked her, and she said,

"_____!" I can't wait to go trick-or-treating!

BONUS: Can you also find the pencil and snake?

Goopy Scoops

The big day is here! The annual neighborhood _____-carving

contest. I have big plans. I want to turn my pumpkin into a replica

of a _____. Won't that be spooky?! So today, I cut the top off

of the best _____ I could find. Then I stuck my hand in and

scooped out a giant glob of _____. Ew, it was slimy. I kept on

scooping until I had a pile as tall as a _____. But I still hadn't

scraped every _____ out. I looked around. The girl next to

me was holding a _____ and had started carving. I felt as

frustrated as a _____. That's when a kid handed me a special

curved _____. "It makes the scooping go faster," he said. Did

it ever! Finally, I'm ready to carve. Maybe I'll win first _____

this year!

BONUS: Can you also find the bat, chick, nail, ruler, and hot dog?

Ghostly Games

I have a new favorite game. It's called "Ghosts in the _____."

Of course, I love it. I am a_____, after all. The rules are

pretty simple. Someone is "it" and covers his or her _____

with a_____. Everyone else hides. They can scrunch down

behind a _____ or even climb up a _____. Then the

_____ who is "it" tries to find everyone. Tonight's game was

epic. My best friend Gertie was "it." Instead of searching for the

rest of us, she lay down on a _____ and closed her eyes. Soon,

she was snoring as loud as a raging _____ . The rest of us

couldn't believe it. We figured it was safe to come out. But when we

did, Gertie yelled, "Awesome _____!" and tagged us all.

BONUS: Can you also find the tooth, mushroom, yo-yo, and snake?

Cauldron Contest

This is a witch's favorite time of year. The time when she can

pull out her biggest _____ from storage and fill it with

goodies—things like a slice of rotten _____, one giant oozing

_____, and essence of _____. This year, Halloween

Town is having a fun _____ cooking contest. The only rule is

that the judge has to taste a pinch of _____ in each cauldron.

But an angry _____ stole the last bag of it months ago.

Thankfully, a young witch named Wanda _____ followed the

thief and saw him hide the bag in an old _____. The night

before the contest, Wanda scurried off. She found the secret stash

and brought some to each _____ in town. The next day,

Wanda won "Worst Batch"—that is witch language for first place!

BONUS: Can you also find the ice-cream bar, present, umbrella, candle, and bird?

The Spooky Salon

Don't let your fur, hair, or _____ look unruly on Halloween.

Grab your _____ and get down to Hair Today right now. We

are having a gruesome sale on _____ waxing and trimming.

One _____ for the price of two! Ha! Just kidding. We'll give

you ten. Remember, we use only the most spoiled ingredients in our

patented "Ugly _____ Lotion." It just costs one _____!

And we know you'll want to smell your nastiest for _____-or-

treating, so our special perfume, Odor of _____, is half off! It

also doubles as food for your pet _____. Yes, there's nothing

like Hair Today for the holiday. All monsters want the very best for

themselves. You won't find that here—but we will give you a free

furry _____ with every visit.

BONUS: Can you also find the ice-cream cone, hammer, fork, and shuttlecock?

Happy Hauntings

"We wish you a merry _____!" OK, I know you usually sing

that song in December as a Christmas _____. But October

31st is my favorite _____ ever, so I changed the words. I'm

going trick-or-treating tonight. I hope I get a chocolate-covered

_____ and a salted-caramel _____. I wouldn't even

mind putting my teeth into a sour _____. I don't know what

to expect from our new neighbors. They moved into the huge

old _____ down the street from us. When I was a little

_____, I thought it was haunted. No one has lived there for

years. Until now. I felt a little nervous, but when I rang the door

_____, a very nice _____ came to the door. Whew.

Nothing spooky here! Merry Halloween to you!

BONUS: Can you also find the tack, needle, sock, spoon, ladder, and banana?

Art by Michael Palan

A Ghostly Outing

I am a ghost, and this is the first year I'm allowed to go trick-or-

treating. Mom has always said, "You are a _____. You aren't

supposed to go trick-or-treating. You are supposed to frighten

every _____ on the street." "But, Mom," I'd whine, "I want to

eat a _____ like every other kid!" So finally, she gave in. I'm

about to ring my first _____. I can hear someone coming

to the _____ right now. I shout, "Trick or _____!"

And then I scream for real. What I see is more frightening than

a _____ wearing a clean _____! But then I see that

the creature is scared of me, too. "Er, _____ or treat?" I ask

quietly. The creature plops a _____ in my basket. We smile at

each other. I can't wait to see what the next house brings!

BONUS: Can you also find the carrot, pencil, and ruler?

Perfect Party

Each Halloween, my cousin Amanda throws a big _____

party. It is the best! We play pin the _____ on the

_____. We have a _____-eating contest. And of course,

we do the _____ dance. But my favorite part is that everyone

gets to carve a _____. This year, I want to give mine a face

like my pet _____. But when I arrive at Amanda's, I see

that the party room is already full of carved jack-o'-lanterns. I feel

disappointed. "What's the _____?" she asks. When I tell her,

she smiles. "Don't worry!" she says. "There are lots more to carve

out in the back _____." Yes! I give her a high-five and race

out back. Like I said, there's no better _____ than Amanda's.

◂ ◦ ▸
BONUS: Can you also find the banana, hockey stick, fish, and envelope?

Monster Town News

Here on Channel _____, we just found out that there has

been a candy burglary at Crystal's _____ Shop, the biggest

candy store in Monster Town! The creepy crooks got away with

every chocolate _____ bar, every piece of _____

gum, and every sugarcoated _____. I suspect that crusty

villain, Cheesy Mc_____. He's been angry ever since Crystal

stopped selling his cheddar-covered _____ bites. But she had

no choice: they were infested with those nasty _____ beetles!

Hold on, this just came in over the MonsterNet: Crystal found the

missing _____! Turns out, she forgot she had donated it to

the town's Halloween party. Well, all's well that ends well. Now, let's

look at that _____ forecast again.

BONUS: Can you also find the matchstick, snake, and screw?

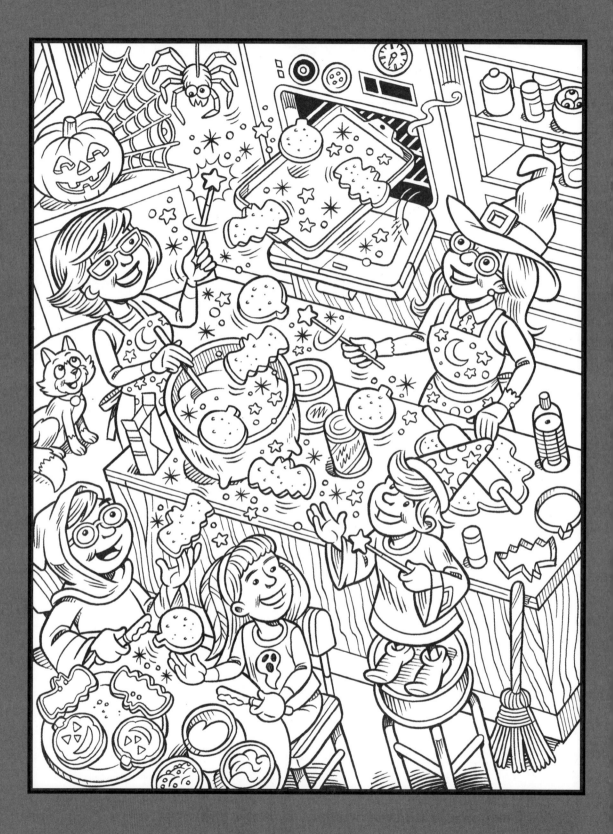

Witch Cookies?

My family is proof that even witches like to bake from scratch. We

don't just point a magic _____ at a pan and expect a perfect

buttery _____ to pop out. Nope, we enjoy mixing each cup

of _____ and every teaspoon of _____ to create our

special Halloween _____ cookies. I confess—we do use a

little magic. Like tonight—my aunt suggested we hold a contest to

see who could get their _____ to hover in the air the longest.

It came down to my little brother and our mom. Mom was so

close, but then her _____ cookie plopped onto our furry pet

_____. My brother got to fly around the _____ as his

prize. Lucky him! I'm not too jealous, though. Tonight is Halloween,

which means I get to fly on my brand-new _____. Lucky me!

BONUS: Can you also find the banana, iron, golf club, and envelope?

Confessions of a Dog

Everyone in my family seems to think that Purrkins the Cat painted

the "Mona _____" and climbed Mount _____—all in

the same day. Sure, she's cute. But dogs—like me—deserve more

respect. Specifically, I deserve a giant _____ covered with

cheese to eat, a soft fuzzy _____ to sleep on, and more

scratches on the top of my _____. But my owner Katy is

carving a giant _____ into an image of Purrkins! Now, here

comes Katy's brother carrying a big _____. Is he going

to carve another _____ of Purrkins?! Wait. Hold on. That

looks like my _____. Could it be?! YES! It is a hot-diggity

_____ pumpkin! Like I always say, "Dogs rule. Cats drool."

Except Purrkins. I confess, I kind of like that kitty.

BONUS: Can you also find the eyeglasses, clothespin, pine cone, and wedge of lemon?

Halloween Camp

I had never heard of Halloween Camp before this summer. I was

nervous. Would I find another _____ to talk to? Would I

sleep OK on a strange _____? And would they have my

favorite food, mac-and-_____? It turned out, I didn't need

to worry. Camp was great! We worked all week to create our own

_____ to wear trick-or-treating. Then on the last day, we

each grabbed a _____ to put candy in, and we knocked on

every _____ at the camp. Counselors gave us a lot of sweet

_____ bars. Then we went back to the main _____

and had a Halloween party. There were games and tons of crafts to

make. I created a _____ out of dried-up _____ chips. It

was a happy, hot Halloween!

BONUS: Can you also find the worm, muffin, screwdriver, ruler, star, flower, slice of watermelon, potato, pencil, key, pizza, and seashell?

The Monster 5-K

It's Halloween day, and every ghoul and _____ in town is

over at Grizzly _____ Park for the annual 5-K race. The *K*

stands for "Kooky." Each year, the town holds a contest to find the

five kookiest monsters to run along the dirt _____ through

the deep, dark _____. This year's racers include a witch

flying on a brown _____ and a young werewolf with only

one _____ on her left foot! This year's grand prize is a meal

at The Cackling _____ Cafeteria. Who wouldn't want that?!

I am rooting for my best _____, Belinda Bat. But no matter

who comes in first _____, all five are already winners. They

are the kookiest monsters in _____ Town, after all. Happy

Halloween to everyone!

BONUS: Can you also find the needle and worm?

Stargazing

What's your favorite constellation? Mine has to be the _____

constellation. You can see it best on a clear October night. I take

my telescope, the _____ 3000, outside and point it at the

sky. I can see everything as clear as a _____! There's the

full moon, with craters that look like a _____. There are

the planets Blue _____ and _____ IX. The brightest

star in the sky, Alpha _____, shines right above me. I even

see a shooting star, and I make a wish that we'll have my favorite

for dinner: spaghetti and _____! Finally, I find my favorite

constellation. "_____!" I exclaim. What a _____ night!

BONUS: Can you also find the hatchet, pushpin, saw, and snake?

Spooky Bowling

Have you ever been to spooky bowling? It is a ghoulishly

_____ good time! Lily invited my sister and me to a party

at Raven's _____ Bowling Alley. We put on our costumes

and hopped in our parents' _____ car. When we walked in,

we were amazed at the _____ decorations everywhere! A

_____ hung from the ceiling in cobwebs, a large spider with

a _____ sat on top of the bowling balls, and the bowling balls

looked like pumpkins with _____ faces! Spooky _____

music played over the _____ speakers. We immediately

joined all our costumed friends, ready to play some _____

games!

BONUS: Can you also find the carrot?

Gecko-ween!

Halloween night was approaching faster than a _____,

and I didn't have a costume yet. Every day in school, I sat at

my_____ and listened to my friends talk about their

_____ plans. There would be witches, superheroes, and

even a character from the popular show, _____ *and the*

_____! I wanted to be something no other _____ would

be. But what? That night, I drew ideas in my _____. I glanced

up and saw my pet gecko, Mr. _____, looking at me from his

_____. That was it! Halloween night came, and I dressed in

my bright, spotted costume. "How do I look?" I asked my gecko. No

one else would be dressed like the best pet in the _____!

BONUS: Can you also find the comb, mushroom,
ring, hockey stick, and pencil?

Monster Mash

Welcome, every _____, to the six hundredth annual Monster

Mash Off, sponsored by _____ Potatoes and More. These

monsters have spent all year perfecting their mashed _____

potato recipes in the hopes of winning the _____ Trophy.

What amazing _____ skills these contestants are displaying

today. Look at Spike, using his great _____ fists to mash

every potato. And no potato is left unpeeled with Armand's many

_____ hands at work. Oh, _____! Webster has gone to

the fridge for his secret ingredient—a _____! Yum! We can't

wait to taste every _____ dish.

BONUS: Can you also find the lightning bolt and tack?

The Largest Pumpkin

How big was the largest _____ you've ever seen? Well, at the

_____ Town Annual _____ Farm Show, the pumpkins

are huge! Every year, farmers from all over the _____

area bring their pumpkins in trucks, boats, and even a hot-air

_____! This year, Farmer Barry _____ tied his down

with a _____ to the back of his _____ truck. He didn't

want it to roll away like last year! Pumpkins are judged by their

color, their shape, and their weight. The winner gets a ginormous

_____! Last year, Farmer Joy won with her 300-pound

_____ pumpkin. What a joy!

BONUS: Can you also find the butter knife, nail, hockey stick, and pencil?

Campfire Tales

Jack tells the best scary stories! Every Friday night out behind the

_____ field, there's a bonfire. Young monsters come to roast

their _____ and listen to Jack's stories. I love going to the

bonfire with my friends, Skelly and Frankie. My parents drive us

there in their _____ car, and we sit down on _____

pumpkins. "Gather 'round, every _____," Jack will start, "and

listen to this _____-chilling tale!" With every _____

word, we get more and more scared, shivering right down to our

_____. Sometimes we'll even scream, "_____!" It really

is the best part of the _____ season!

BONUS: Can you also find the hammer, hockey stick, and slice of cake?

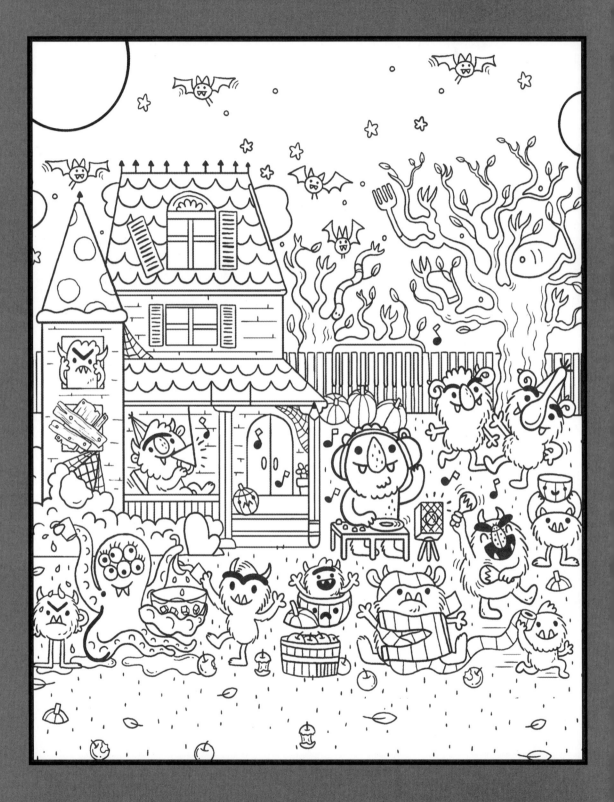

Monster's Bash

Food, games, and music, oh my! It was time for the annual

Monster's Bash! DJ_____ Bones played the best songs,

including hits like "_____ Mash" and "_____-busters."

When I heard my favorite song, "I Put a _____ On You," I

put down my cup of _____ berry punch and ran to show off

my dance moves. Some monsters played games like bobbing for

a _____ and the mummy wrap, in which teams compete to

wrap a player in a _____ like a mummy. Little Jack got a bit

too enthusiastic and kept wrapping and wrapping and wrapping

until Harry looked like a _____! We partied well into the

night, until the _____ rose in the sky. What a _____

party!

BONUS: Can you also find the comb, fork, letter *E*, pair of pants, pencil, question mark, slice of pizza, sock, toothbrush, ice-cream cone, and fish?

Spook-tacular Halloween!

Use the extra stickers to fill in the blanks!

Halloween night was almost over. My brother and I were dressed

in the best costumes ever. I was the superhero The Great

_____ and he was a cow-_____! We had been to

almost every _____ house in our town. Our bags were

stuffed with chocolate and _____ bars. But there was still

one more house! It was at the edge of _____ Town, and

the decorations were amazing. A giant _____ spider hung

from a tree. A skeleton holding a _____ sat by the door.

Spooky _____ music came from inside the house. We were

almost too scared to knock on the _____. But we did, and

we received the tastiest _____ bars!

What a great Halloween!

Answers

▼ Page 4

▼ Page 6

▼ Page 8

▼ Page 10

▼ Page 12

▼ Page 14

▼ Page 16

▼ Page 18

Answers

▼ Page 20

▼ Page 22

▼ Page 24

▼ Page 26

▼ Page 28

▼ Page 30

▼ Page 32

▼ Page 34

▼ Page 36